C·O·O·K·I·N·G
step by step

DK | Penguin Random House

Senior Editor James Mitchem
Senior Designer Elaine Hewson
Art Direction for Photography Charlotte Bull
Designers Charlotte Bull, Samantha Richiardi
Editorial Assistance Sally Beets, Carrie Love
Photographer Dave King
Home Economist and Food Stylist Denise Smart
Recipe Tester Sue Davie
Pre-Production Producer Tony Phipps
Senior Producer John Casey
Jacket Designer Charlotte Bull
Jacket Co-ordinator Francesca Young
Creative Technical Support Sonia Charbonnier
Managing Editor Penny Smith
Managing Art Editor Mabel Chan
Publisher Mary Ling
Art Director Jane Bull

First published in Great Britain in 2018 by
Dorling Kindersley Limited
80 Strand, London, WC2R 0RL

Copyright © 2018 Dorling Kindersley Limited
A Penguin Random House Company
10 9 8 7 6 5 4 3 2 1
001–305620–Feb/2018

A CIP catalogue record for this book
is available from the British Library.
ISBN: 978-0-2413-0037-4

Printed in China

A WORLD OF IDEAS:
SEE ALL THERE IS TO KNOW

www.dk.com

C·O·O·K·I·N·G
step by step

Contents

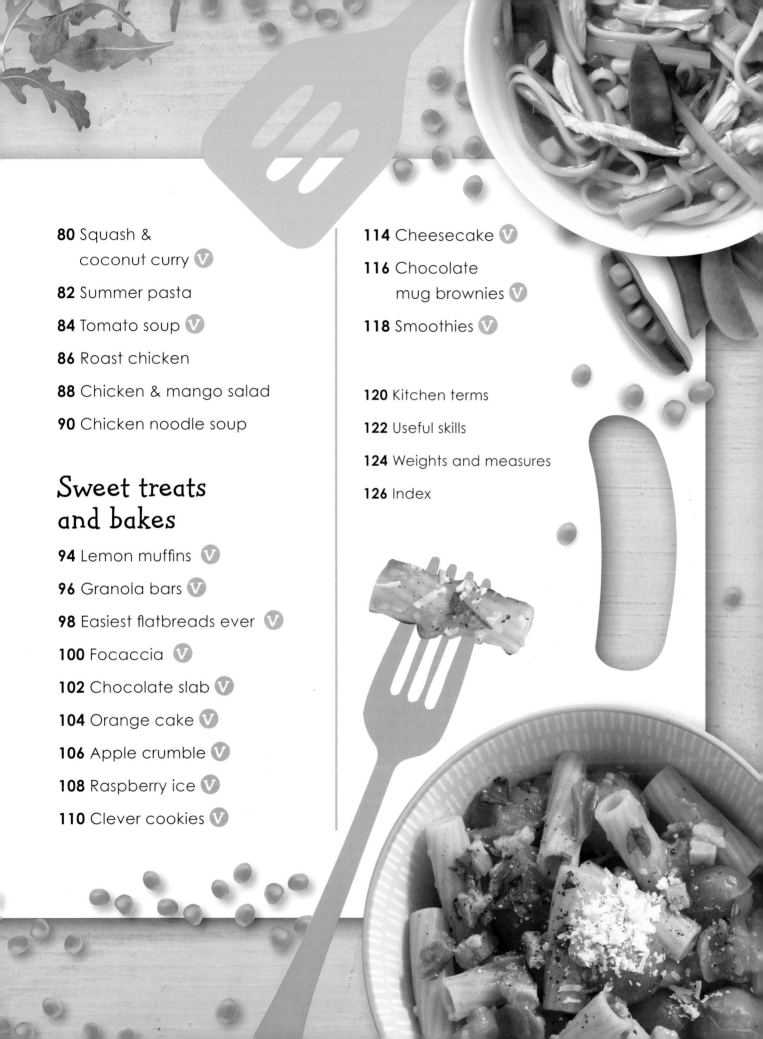

Kitchen rules

Even the most experienced cooks need to follow kitchen rules. So whether you're new to cooking or not, be sure to follow these guidelines so everyone is safe, healthy, and ready to have fun.

Hygiene

Being clean and careful in the kitchen will prevent germs from spreading, and stop you from getting poorly.

• Always wash your hands before you begin cooking, and wash them again if they get messy, or if you touch raw meat, fish, or poultry.

• Use hot soapy water to clean chopping boards and knives used to cut raw meat, fish, or poultry.

• Be sure to check use-by dates on ingredients.

• All fruits and vegetables should be washed before you begin cooking with them.

• Tasting as you cook is part of the fun, but never try something containing uncooked meat, fish, poultry, or eggs.

Safety

Cooking is great fun, but it can also be dangerous. Use these steps to make sure you don't hurt yourself.

• Always have an adult around while you cook so they can watch out for you and help with the trickier or more dangerous parts.

• Ask an adult to help whenever you need to touch anything hot.

• Take extra special care when cutting, peeling, grating, or using a blender.

• Tidy up as you go and be sure to wipe up any spillages.

This symbol means you need to take extra care as the instructions involve something sharp or hot.

Getting started

In this book, you'll find lots of simple, delicious, and fun recipes to make. But before you get started, take a few minutes to read about how best to prepare.

Before you start cooking

- Read each recipe all the way through before you begin; you don't want to get halfway through and realize you've forgotten a key ingredient.

- Gather all the equipment and ingredients together.

- Tie back long hair, roll up sleeves, and put an apron on.

Look out for these symbols:

Serves
How many people the dish serves, or how many portions it makes.

Cooking
How long the meal takes to cook.

5 mins   30 mins   Serves 4

These times are just guides, so use your judgement if you think a dish needs more time in the oven.

Preparation
How long preparation takes (includes chilling, freezing, and marinating).

Imperial measures

oz = ounce
lb = pound
fl oz = fluid ounce

Tip:
If you get stuck when following a recipe, or aren't sure what a word means, flip to the back of this book to find a handy glossary of kitchen terms.

Weights and measures

You'll find the ingredients you need for every dish clearly listed on each recipe. Measure them out before you begin. Here's a guide to what the abbreviations stand for:

Spoon measures

tsp = teaspoon
tbsp = tablespoon

Metric measures

g = gram
ml = millilitre

Other important things you need to know

Seasoning

If a recipe suggests adding seasoning, this means you can add salt or pepper. Use just a little at a time so you don't put in too much.

Using the oven

Preheat your oven for at least 15 minutes before using it so that it reaches the recommended temperature. Also, remember that cooking times can vary depending on the oven or pan you are using.

Vegetarian dishes (V)

Look for this symbol on the contents page to find recipes suitable for vegetarians.

Variations

Some recipes in this book include suggested alternate options to the basic recipe, but don't be afraid to think of your own versions, too!

Equipment

Here's a list of equipment you'll need to make the recipes in the book. Before you cook a dish, read the recipe and gather up what you need.

Serving and dipping bowls

Heatproof bowls

Mixing bowls

Scales

Measuring jug

Measuring cups

Plastic tub

Wooden spoon

Serving spoon

Pastry brush

Knife

Fork

Tablespoon

Teaspoon

Measuring spoons

Spatula

Ladle

Garlic press

Frying pans

Griddle pan

Large saucepan (with lid)

Small saucepan (with lid)

Wok

Baking paper

Clingfilm

Tin foil

Kitchen paper

Electric whisk

Microwave

The brownies on page 116 need to be cooked in a microwave.

Stick blender

Food processor

Blender

Peeler

Pizza cutter

Grater

Potato masher

Skewers

Sieves

Whisk

Rolling pin

Tongs

Muffin cases

Cooling rack

Chopping board

Muffin tin

Roasting tin

Baking beans

Baking trays

Quiche tin

Ovenproof dish

Baking sheets

Cake tins

Light bites

These tempting recipes are
a mix of quick, simple snacks,
or dishes that are perfect for
sharing with your friends.

Ingredients

500g (1lb 2oz) mixed berries + 6 tbsp caster sugar + 1 tsp vanilla extract + 150ml (5fl oz) milk +

Fluffy pancakes

Pancakes are the ultimate breakfast treat, especially with this berry compote. If you're short on time, just use regular fruit and top with yogurt, honey, or maple syrup.

Gooey fruit

Make a stack!

15 mins   10 mins   Makes 8-10

 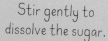 

1 egg, lightly beaten	+	2 tbsp melted butter	+	125g (4½oz) plain flour	+	1 tsp baking powder	+	1 tbsp sunflower oil

1

Stir gently to dissolve the sugar.

⚠️

Place the berries, 2 tbsp of sugar, and vanilla extract in a pan and bring to the boil. Simmer for 3-5 minutes and set aside.

2

Wet

Dry

Whisk the milk, egg, and butter in a jug. Sift the flour, remaining sugar, baking powder, and a pinch of salt into a bowl. Beat the wet ingredients into the dry.

3

Watch for the bubbles!

⚠️

Heat a non-stick pan over a medium heat. Add a little oil to the pan and spoon in a 2 tbsp of the mixture per pancake. Cook for 2-3 minutes.

4

Add a little oil to the pan between batches to prevent sticking.

⚠️

Once bubbles appear, flip the pancakes and cook for a further 2 minutes. Keep the pancakes warm in the oven while you make the rest.

15

Omelettes

A perfect omelette should be creamy, not rubbery. To achieve this, cook it over a low heat.

Ingredients

2 large eggs + ½ tsp butter

1

Break the eggs into a small bowl. Season with salt and pepper then whisk together with a fork.

Cheese

25g (scant 1oz) Cheddar or Gruyère cheese

Variations

One of the best things about omelettes is they're easy to adapt. By adding these extra ingredients before folding, you can make several variations.

Mushroom

4 button mushrooms, chopped, cooked, and seasoned

2

Heat the butter in a non-stick pan until foamy. Add the beaten egg and swirl with a spatula. Tilt the pan to let the egg run into any gaps.

3

Continue cooking for 30 seconds, or until set around the edges. Add any fillings then carefully fold the omelette in half.

Vegetable

1 slice ham, chopped

1 tomato, finely sliced

3 tbsp cooked peas

Handful of fresh spinach leaves

60g (2oz) roasted red pepper

Ham & tomato

Crunchy coating

Serve with a dip of your choice.

Chicken goujons

This recipe is about preparation. All you need to do is move the chicken from one bowl to the next to create a delicious, crunchy coating.

15 mins   25 mins   Serves 4

Ingredients

50g (1¾oz) plain flour   +   1 tsp paprika   +   2 eggs   +

1

Preheat the oven to 190°C (375°F/Gas 5). Mix the flour and paprika in a bowl and season.

To stop the flour clumping on your fingers, use one hand to dip into the flour and breadcrumbs, and the other to dip into the eggs.

2

Beat 2 eggs in a second bowl.

3

Combine the breadcrumbs and parsley in a third bowl.

4

Dip the chicken into each bowl in the order shown here, then place on an oiled tray and bake for 20-25 minutes.

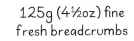
125g (4½oz) fine fresh breadcrumbs

+

2 tbsp freshly chopped parsley

+

4 boneless, skinless chicken breasts, cut into strips

+

2 tbsp sunflower oil

Sweet potato fries

Crispy, herby, and very tasty, these sweet potato fries make a great side dish or snack.

Crispy fries

10 mins plus 1 hr soaking   30 mins   Serves 4

Ingredients

2 sweet potatoes, about 500g (1lb 2oz)

2 tbsp olive oil

2 tsp dried mixed herbs

1 tbsp polenta or cornmeal

sea salt

You can peel the potatoes if you like, but you don't have to.

1

Cut the potatoes into 5mm (¼in) sticks and soak in cold water for 1 hour. Drain and pat dry with a tea towel.

2

Dried potatoes

Preheat the oven to 220°C (425°F/Gas 7). Mix the herbs and polenta together.

3

Drizzle oil over the potatoes and add the polenta mixture. Toss to coat and spread out on a non-stick baking tray.

4

Soaking the potatoes removes starch, and helps make them crispy.

Bake in the oven for about 30 minutes, turning once, until crispy. Sprinkle with sea salt, and serve.

21

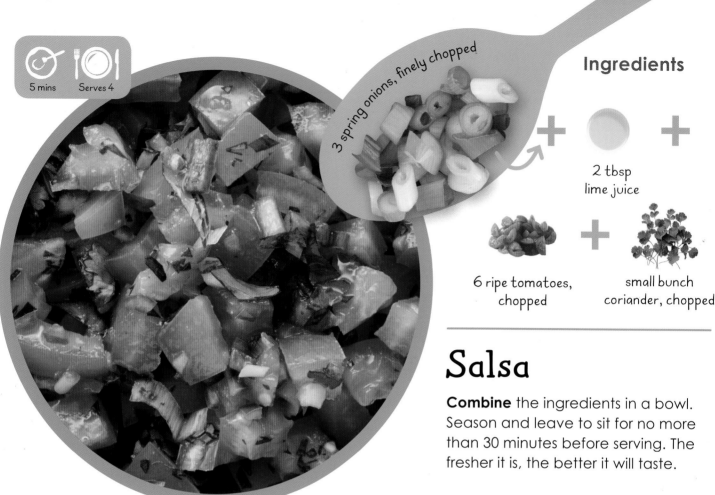

3 spring onions, finely chopped

Ingredients

2 tbsp
lime juice

6 ripe tomatoes,
chopped

small bunch
coriander, chopped

Salsa

Combine the ingredients in a bowl. Season and leave to sit for no more than 30 minutes before serving. The fresher it is, the better it will taste.

Add a drizzle of oil
and a sprinkle of paprika
(optional).

Houmous

Place all the ingredients in a food processor and blitz for 30 second intervals, scraping down the sides as needed. Add seasoning and 2-3 tbsp water and blend until smooth. Transfer to a bowl.

½ tsp ground cumin

Ingredients

400g (14oz) can
chickpeas, drained

3 tbsp
lemon juice

4 tbsp tahini
paste

1 garlic clove,
crushed

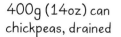

22

5 mins   Serves 4

Ingredients

½ cucumber, peeled and deseeded

200g (7oz) Greek yoghurt

1 tbsp lemon juice

1 garlic clove, crushed

1 tbsp freshly chopped mint

Tzatziki

Grate the cucumber and use kitchen paper to squeeze out excess water. Mix in a bowl with the rest of the ingredients. Chill before serving.

2 avocados, destoned and chopped

Guacamole

Place the ingredients in a bowl and crush with a fork or potato masher. Mash until combined, leaving some larger avocado chunks. Season to taste.

4 tbsp freshly chopped coriander

1 tbsp lime juice

1 small tomato, finely chopped

Gazpacho

A chilled tomato and cucumber soup from Spain, Gazpacho is very refreshing on a hot summer day.

Add chopped spring onions, parsley, and cucumber.

Ingredients

 +  +  + +

100g (3½oz) crusty bread

2 tbsp red wine vinegar

1kg (2¼lb) ripe tomatoes, chopped

1 red and 1 green pepper, deseeded and roughly chopped

1

Vinegar helps bring out the flavour of the tomatoes.

Tear up the bread and place in a bowl. Pour the vinegar on top and leave to soak for 10 minutes.

2

Do this in two batches and store the mixture in a jug.

Blend half the tomatoes, peppers, and cucumber with half the garlic and oil in a food processor for 1 minute, then add half the bread and blend until smooth.

3

Repeat with the remaining ingredients and season to taste.

4

Pass the mixture through a sieve into a large bowl, then cover and refrigerate until chilled before serving.

 +  +

1 cucumber, peeled and roughly chopped

2 garlic cloves, peeled and crushed

120ml (4fl oz) extra virgin olive oil

2 x 400g (14oz) cans
chickpeas, drained

+

1 clove garlic,
crushed

+

2 tsp ground
cumin

+

1 tsp ground
coriander

+

Baked falafel

15 mins plus
25 mins chilling   15 mins   Serves 4

Crunchy, fluffy, and tasty – falafel are a popular
Middle Eastern dish. Falafel are usually fried, but
these baked ones are easier to make.

Yogurt dip

Serve with warm
pitta, salad, and a
yogurt dip.

+  + +  +

2 tbsp freshly chopped flat-leaf parsley — 1 tsp baking powder — 2 tbsp lemon juice — 2 tbsp plain flour — 1 tbsp olive oil, plus extra for brushing

1

⚠ **Pulse** the chickpeas, garlic, spices, and herbs. Season, then pulse in a food processor until chopped.

2

⚠ **Add** the baking powder, lemon juice, flour, and oil. Pulse again until well combined.

3

⚠ **Divide** the mixture into 16 balls and flatten. Cover and chill in the fridge for 25 minutes. Preheat the oven to 190°C (375°F/Gas 5).

4

⚠ **Place** on an oiled baking tray and cook for 10 minutes. Then turn them over and cook for another 5-10 minutes.

For the dip:
- 100g (3½oz) natural yogurt
- 2 tbsp freshly chopped mint
- ¼ cucumber, finely chopped

Ingredients

400g (14oz) peeled
butternut squash, cubed

+

1 courgette, cut into
2.5cm (1in) chunks

+

1 red onion, cut
into 8 wedges

+

1 red pepper, deseeded and
cut into 2.5cm (1in) pieces

+

Roasted veg & couscous salad

Serve this healthy dish warm as
a main, or cold as a side dish
with grilled chicken or fish.

15 mins   40 mins   Serves 4

2

Try to get all the
vegetables in one layer.

1

Preheat the oven to 200°C (400°F/Gas 6).
Scatter the squash, courgette, onion,
and pepper into a roasting tray.
Drizzle with olive oil and season.

Roast for 15 minutes, then turn the vegetables
over so they cook evenly. Return to the oven
and cook for a further 15-20 minutes.

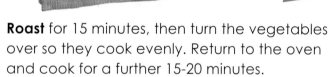

3

Place the couscous in a large bowl and
add the stock, lemon zest, and juice. Stir,
cover, and leave to stand for 5 minutes.
Season to taste and fluff with a fork.

 1 tbsp olive oil

+

200g (7oz) couscous

+

300ml (10fl oz) hot vegetable stock

+

zest and juice of 2 lemons

+

4 tbsp freshly chopped mixed herbs

4

Mix the vegetables and herbs into the couscous.

Great to eat hot or cold!

Crispy chickpeas

These baked chickpeas are a simple snack. The base recipe just has salt and pepper, but you can add more flavourings to switch things up.

1

Preheat the oven to 200°C (400°F/Gas 6). Place the chickpeas on a rimmed baking tray and dry them with kitchen paper and remove any loose skins.

5 mins   30 mins   Serves 4-6

For variations

Cook the chickpeas as above, adding the flavourings before returning to the oven to crisp for the last 30 minutes.

2 tsp dried mixed herbs

Moroccan

Herby Parmesan

3 tbsp grated Parmesan

2

Mix the oil, salt, and pepper in a bowl and pour onto the chickpeas. Stir to coat.

3

Roast for 30 minutes, stirring once to ensure even cooking. Turn off the oven and leave in there for 30 minutes to crisp up.

Ingredients

2 x 400g (14oz) cans chickpeas, drained and rinsed + 1 tbsp olive oil + 2 tsp sea salt + 1 tsp ground black pepper

Salt & Pepper

2 tbsp Moroccan spice mixture

Honey & cinnamon

For this variation, don't include the salt and pepper.

1 tsp ground cinnamon and 2 tbsp honey

Lunch wraps

A great alternative to sandwiches, wraps can be filled with your favourite ingredients. These ones are easy to make, but first you'll need to do a little prep.

Wraps make great healthy packed lunches.

Take extra special care cutting vegetab

32

Pepper

1

Slice off the top and pull out the seeds.

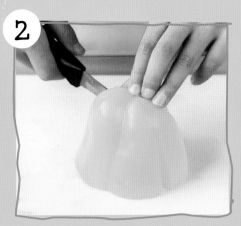

2

Cut into four sections.

Keep your fingers tucked away safely.

3

Trim any pith and slice into thin strips.

Carrot

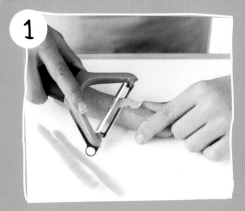

1

Peel a carrot and cut off the top and bottom.

2

Chop the carrot into medium-sized chunks.

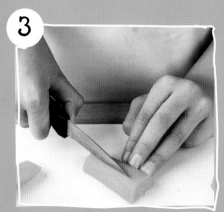

3

Slice the chunks lengthwise into sticks.

Beetroot

1

Cut a cooked beetroot in half.

2

Cut each half into slices.

Beetroot can be a little messy, so watch out!

3

Slice into smaller pieces.

Ingredients

| large tortilla wrap | cream cheese | handful of baby spinach leaves | 1 beetroot, cooked and sliced | ½ pepper, sliced | ½ carrot, sliced |

Rolling your wraps

5 mins · Makes 1

Take your prepped vegetables and roll them up as shown. Then try the recipes on the next page, or create your own wrap recipe.

1 **Spread** a layer of cream cheese onto a tortilla.

2 **Arrange** your rainbow of chopped vegetables on top.

Ready to eat!

3 **Fold** in three edges of the tortilla.

4 **Roll** from the closed end to close the wrap.

5 **Slice** in half.

34

large tortilla wrap

mayonnaise

2 slices
bacon, cooked

handful of
lettuce leaves

3 cherry
tomatoes, halved

BLT

This crispy wrap is a great alternative to the classic BLT sandwich. Do you know what "BLT" stands for? It means bacon, lettuce, and tomato!

5 mins   Makes 1

Houmous avocado

This yummy wrap is full of healthy greens that go perfectly with the creamy houmous.

5 mins   Makes 1

Ingredients

large tortilla wrap

houmous

avocado, peeled
and cut into strips

¼ cucumber,
sliced

handful of
rocket leaves

Ingredients

4 large beefsteak tomatoes,
about 250g (9oz) each

1 tsp salt

2 tbsp olive oil

1 small onion,
chopped

Stuffed tomatoes

15 mins · 45 mins · Makes 4

Vegetables stuffed with meat are popular in
lots of countries. This version comes from France,
where it is called *Tomates farcies*.

Tomato hats!

Cook the tomatoes
in a roasting dish
to catch the juices.

1 clove garlic,
crushed

450g (1lb) good
quality sausages

4 tbsp chopped
parsley

2 tsp chopped
thyme

The salt
draws out
excess liquid.

1

Ask an adult to cut a 2cm (¾in) thick slice off the top of the tomatoes and scoop out the insides. Save the tops for later.

2

Sprinkle salt into the tomatoes and turn them upside down. Meanwhile heat 1 tbsp of oil in a small pan and cook the onion and garlic over low heat for 2-3 minutes until soft.

3

Preheat the oven to 200°C (400°F/Gas 6). Squeeze the meat out of the sausage skins into a bowl. Mix in the onion, garlic, herbs, then season.

4

Rinse out the salt, then stuff the mixture into the tomatoes. Put the tops back on, drizzle with the remaining oil, and cook for 45 minutes.

Ingredients

2 small avocados, diced

\+

2 tbsp fresh coriander, chopped

\+

2 tbsp lime juice

\+

2 tbsp olive oil

\+

Quesadillas

 5 mins   10 mins   Serves 2

Gooey quesadillas are quick to make and totally tasty. These are filled with black beans and avocado, but there are two delicious variations to try on the next page.

1

Lime juice stops the avocado from turning brown.

Mash the avocado, coriander, and lime juice in a bowl. Season with salt and pepper and set aside.

2

Heat half the oil in a pan over medium heat and cook the onion and pepper for 2-3 minutes until softened.

3

Add the beans, season, then cook for about 2 minutes and set aside.

4

Spread half the avocado mixture onto half of one of the tortillas, then top with the pepper and bean mixture.

½ red onion, sliced

 ½ red pepper, sliced

 ½ x 400g (14oz) can black beans, drained

 2 flour tortillas

 50g (1¾oz) Cheddar cheese, grated

Serve with salsa.

5 Repeat with the other tortilla and sprinkle cheese on top. Fold both tortillas in half to make half moon shapes.

6 Heat the remaining oil over low heat and fry the quesadillas for 2 minutes each side, or until golden brown.

The half moon shapes keep the filling from falling out when flipping.

Ingredients

 +  + + +

| 2 flour tortillas | 1 tbsp olive oil | 1 potato, cut into cubes | 1 onion, chopped | 100g (3½oz) diced chorizo | 75g (2½oz) Cheddar cheese, grated |

More quesadillas

5 mins   15 mins   Serves 2

Once you know how to make quesadillas you can get creative with the fillings. After you try these two, why not come up with your own versions?

Chorizo & potato

Heat the oil in a pan and cook the potato for 10 minutes, until softened. Add the onion and chorizo and cook for a further 2-3 minutes. Fill and cook as on the previous page.

Chicken & sweetcorn

Spread the salsa onto one half of each tortilla and top with the rest of the ingredients. Cook the quesadillas as you did on the previous page.

5 mins | 5 mins | Serves 2

Ingredients

2 flour tortillas + 4 tbsp salsa + 75g (2½oz) leftover chicken from page 86 + 50g (1¾oz) sweetcorn + ½ red pepper, chopped + 75g (2½oz) Cheddar cheese, grated

500g (1lb 2oz) ready prepared shortcrust pastry

+

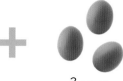

3 eggs

+

150ml (5fl oz) double cream

+

200ml (7fl oz) milk

+

Cheesy quiche

35 mins   45 mins   Serves 6-8

This classic tart originated in France, where it is called *Quiche Lorraine*. It's light and yummy, and a great way to get started using pastry.

Cut into slices and serve with a salad.

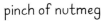

pinch of nutmeg   +   200g (7oz) cooked bacon, chopped   +   100g (3½oz) Gruyère cheese, grated

1

Preheat the oven to 190°C (375°F/Gas 6). Roll out the pastry and line a loose-bottomed 23cm (9in) quiche tin. Chill for 15 minutes and prick with a fork.

2

This is called "blind baking". It stops the pastry getting soggy when the filling is added.

Line with baking paper and fill with baking beans. Place on a baking tray and bake for 15 minutes. Remove the paper and beans and bake for a further 5 minutes.

3

Whisk together the eggs, cream, milk, and nutmeg. Transfer to a jug.

5

Pour the egg mixture on top and sprinkle on the remaining cheese. Bake for 25-30 minutes, then leave to cool for 5 minutes.

4

Scatter the bacon and half of the cheese over the pastry base.

250g (9oz)
plain flour

+

1 tsp
baking powder

+

1 tsp
dried oregano

+

115g (4oz) butter,
melted

+

250ml (9fl oz) milk

Pizza muffins

These easy, cheesy treats are a tasty twist
on pizza. They're great on their own, but
even better with a yummy dipping sauce.

15 mins | 45 mins | Makes 8-10

Sprinkle with
basil.

Dip in
pizza
sauce.

 **2 eggs**

 **2 tbsp pizza sauce, plus extra for dipping**

 115g (4oz) mixed Cheddar and mozzarella cheese, grated

 **150g (5½oz) mini pepperoni, sliced**

1

The butter stops the muffins from sticking.

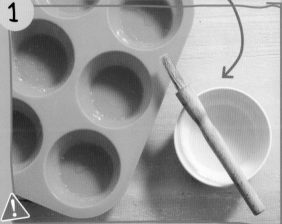

Preheat the oven to 190°C (375°F/Gas 5) and grease a muffin tin with oil.

2

Give it a good mix.

Mix the flour, baking powder, and oregano in a bowl, and the butter, milk, eggs, and pizza sauce in a jug.

3

Pour the egg mixture into the flour mixture and lightly stir together. Then fold in the cheese and pepperoni.

4

Only fill the cups up ¾ of the way or the mix will spill out.

Spoon the mixture into the muffin tin and bake for 20-25 minutes until golden.

Main dishes

There's nothing quite like a delicious, satisfying meal. So learn to cook your favourite dishes and dinner will always feel special.

Ingredients

250g (9oz)
dried macaroni

+

150g (5½oz)
soft cream cheese

+

300ml (10fl oz) milk

+

1 tsp Dijon mustard

+

175g (6oz)
Cheddar cheese, grated

+

8 cherry tomatoes, halved

48

Mac & cheese

Almost everyone loves mac and cheese! And this clever "cheat's" way to make it couldn't be simpler.

5 mins   30 mins   Serves 4

Serve with a crisp green salad.

1 **Preheat** the oven to 190°C (375°F/Gas 5). Cook the pasta in a pan of lightly salted boiling water for 7–9 minutes. Drain and transfer to an ovenproof dish.

2 **Mix** the cream cheese, milk, mustard, and half the Cheddar in a bowl. Season and whisk until smooth.

3 **Pour** the sauce over the pasta and mix. Sprinkle the remaining cheese and tomatoes on top. Cook in the oven for 20 minutes, until golden and bubbly.

49

Fried rice

Making fried rice is a simple and fantastic way to turn leftover rice into something exciting.

1

Heat the oil in a wok. Add the rice, peas, and pepper, and cook for 3-4 minutes.

2

Push the rice mixture to one side and pour the egg into the wok.

3

Let the egg set for 10 seconds, then break it up and stir it into the rice.

5 mins   8 mins   Serves 4

Ingredients

 +
 +
 +
 +

2 tbsp sunflower oil

500g (1lb 2oz) cooked long-grain rice

125g (4½oz) frozen peas

½ red pepper, finely sliced

4

Stir in the corn, onions, beansprouts, and soy sauce, and cook for a further 2-3 minutes.

Packed with flavour!

2 eggs, beaten

125g (4½oz) sweetcorn

4 spring onions, chopped

125g (4½oz) beansprouts

2 tbsp light soy sauce

This will remove excess water from tofu.

1

Place the tofu between two sheets of kitchen paper and put something heavy on top for 15 minutes.

2

Cut the tofu into 2.5cm (1in) cubes and combine with the oil, garlic, lemon juice, vinegar, and herbs. Marinate for 1 hour.

3

Preheat the grill to medium and thread the tofu and vegetables onto skewers.

4

Grill the kebabs for 5-6 minutes then turn and brush with any remaining marinade. Cook for a further 5 minutes.

Ingredients

  +   +   +   +

400g (14oz) firm tofu

2 tbsp olive oil

1 clove garlic, crushed

2 tbsp lemon juice

Tofu kebabs

These kebabs are simple and healthy.
Try varying the vegetables by
adding mushrooms or
cubes of courgette.

15 mins plus
1 hr marinating

10 mins

Makes 4

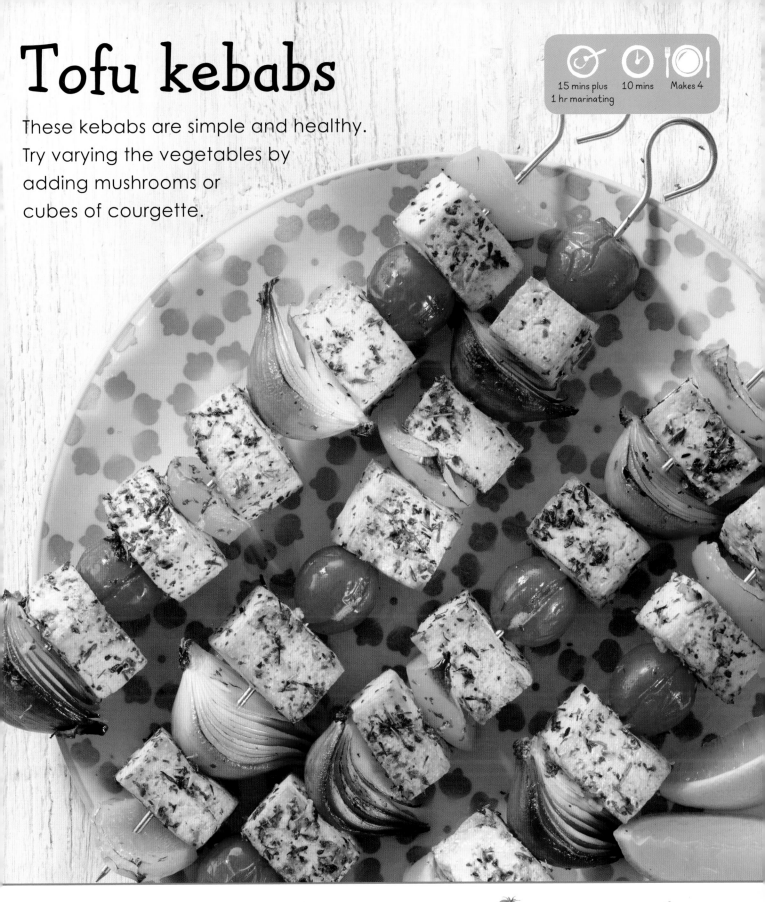

1 tbsp red
wine vinegar

+

2 tsp dried
mixed herbs

+

1 small red onion,
cut into 8 wedges

+

8 cherry tomatoes

+

8 cubes
yellow pepper

53

Ingredients

175g (6oz) strong
white bread flour

+

½ tsp salt

+

½ tsp fast-action
dried yeast

+

120ml (4fl oz)
warm water

+

1 tbsp extra
virgin olive oil

+

2 tbsp pizza sauce

+

25g (scant 1oz) Cheddar
cheese, grated

+

125g (4½oz) mozzarella,
drained and sliced

+

2 tomatoes, sliced

Perfect pizza

It's easy to make pizza from scratch. Here's a basic recipe and a few variations to start with, but there are so many options when it comes to pizza!

1

Combine the flour, salt, and yeast in a bowl. Make a well and add the water and oil.

2

Mix until the dough comes together, then knead for 10 minutes until smooth.

3

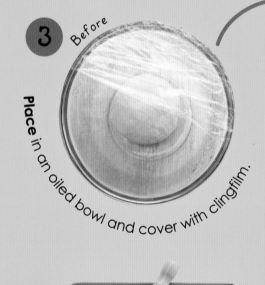

Before / After

Place in an oiled bowl and cover with clingfilm.

Leave to rise for an hour, or until it has doubled in size. Preheat the oven to 220°C (425°C/Gas 7).

4

Place on a lightly greased baking sheet, then roll the dough into a 25cm (10in) circle.

5

Spread on the sauce and top with the cheese and tomatoes. Bake for 10-15 minutes.

Sprinkle
with basil.

Ham & mushroom

Spread pizza sauce on the base and scatter the rest of the ingredients on top. Add optional oregano if you like.

Extra ingredients

50g (1¾oz)
sliced ham

50g (1¾oz)
sliced mushrooms

50g (1¾ oz) Cheddar
cheese, grated

Extra ingredients

50g (1¾oz)
sliced mozzarella

50g (1¾oz)
Gorgonzola

60g (2oz)
ricotta cheese

25g (scant 1oz)
grated Parmesan

Four cheese

Omit the pizza sauce. Layer the mozzarella and Gorgonzola around the base. Top with teaspoons of ricotta, then scatter over the Parmesan.

Pepper & pepperoni

Spread pizza sauce on the base and sprinkle the cheese on top. Add the pepperoni and slices of the peppers.

Extra ingredients

 +

100g (3½oz) grated mozzarella · 100g (3½oz) pepperoni, sliced

+

½ sliced green and red pepper

Extra ingredients

 +

100g (3½oz) baby spinach, wilted · 15g (½oz) grated Parmesan

+

100g (3½oz) ricotta cheese

Spinach & ricotta

Spread the base with pizza sauce and sprinkle with Parmesan. Top with the spinach and spoonfuls of ricotta.

Ingredients

25g (scant 1oz)
butter, softened

+

1 tsp grated
lemon zest

+

1 tbsp freshly
chopped dill

+

50g (1¾oz) green
beans, trimmed

 10 mins
 20 mins
 Serves 2

Salmon parcels

Fish is healthy and delicious, but can be tricky to cook. However, it's super easy if you cook it in baking paper.

The baking paper steams the fish.

Squeeze the lemon over the fish.

 **50g (1¾oz) mangetout or sugar snap peas**

 **50g (1¾oz) baby spinach**

 **2 boneless, skinless salmon fillets**

 2 lemon wedges

 1

 2

Preheat the oven to 200°C (400°F/Gas 6). Cut two large squares of baking paper and mix the butter, lemon zest, and dill.

Stack half the vegetables in the centre of one of the sheets of baking paper and place a piece of salmon on top.

 3

 4

Top with half the butter and a lemon wedge. Then seal the parcel by folding it up and twisting the ends.

Repeat with the other parcel, then cook for 20-25 minutes, until cooked through.

Ingredients

1 onion, sliced

500g (1lb 2oz) mini new potatoes

carrots
400g (14oz) carrots, cut into chunks

200g (7oz) button mushrooms

8 pork sausages

Sausage bake

This hearty dish is so easy to make. All you need to do is add all the ingredients to a pan and let the oven do the rest!

10 mins | 1 hour | Serves 4

One pan wonder!

1

Preheat the oven to 180°C (350°F/Gas 4). Place the onion, potatoes, carrots, and mushrooms into an ovenproof dish.

2

Arrange the sausages on top and drizzle with oil. Mix the stock with the tomato purée and soy or Worcestershire sauce.

3

Pour the stock mixture on top, season, and cook in the oven for 30 minutes. Stir and cook for a further 30 minutes.

+ 1 tbsp olive oil

+ 400ml (14fl oz) hot beef stock

+ 1 tsp tomato purée

+ dash of soy or Worcestershire sauce

Serve with peas, green beans, or broccoli.

Sprinkle with parsley before serving, for extra colour and flavour.

Spiced rice

Cooking rice in a delicious
sauce is a great way to
give it loads of extra flavour.

Top with a
fried egg.

Ingredients

62

| 250g (9oz) long grain rice | + | 2 tbsp vegetable oil | + | 1 onion, finely chopped | + | 2 cloves garlic, crushed | + | 1 green pepper, finely chopped |

1

Cook the rice according to the pack instructions and drain.

2

Heat the oil over medium heat and cook the onion and garlic for 3-4 minutes. Add the pepper and cook for 2-3 minutes.

3

Stir in the cumin, oregano, bay leaf, and tomatoes and cook for 4-5 minutes.

4

Take the bay leaf out before you serve.

Add the passata and cook for 4-5 minutes on low heat. Stir the rice into the sauce

½ tsp ground cumin

1 tsp dried oregano

1 bay leaf

2 tomatoes, chopped

200ml (7fl oz) passata

Caesar salad

5 mins · **20 mins** · **Serves 2**

This classic dish combines delicious chicken, crispy lettuce, crunchy croutons, and a rich, creamy sauce.

Top with shavings of Parmesan cheese.

Preheat the oven to 190°C (375°F/Gas 5). Coat the bread with oil and a little salt.

Bake the bread for about 10 minutes, until it's golden and crunchy.

Cook the chicken in a griddle pan for 7 minutes each side, or until fully cooked through. Cut into strips.

Place the lettuce in a bowl and mix in the dressing, chicken, and bread.

Mix in 1 tbsp of the dressing at a time so you don't add too much.

Ingredients

 +  +  + +

2 slices crusty bread, torn or cut into pieces | 2 tbsp olive oil | 2 small boneless, skinless chicken breasts | 1 Romaine lettuce, chopped | caesar dressing, to serve

65

50g (1¾oz)
pine nuts

2 cloves garlic

1 tsp sea salt

50g (1¾oz)
fresh basil leaves

Pasta with pesto

Fresh pesto is so much better than the jars
from a shop. A fresh batch like this should
keep in the fridge for up to a week.

10 mins   10 mins   Serves 4

Creamy
sauce

Fresh
basil

 +  +  +

125g (4½oz) freshly grated Parmesan cheese + **150ml (5fl oz) extra virgin olive oil** + **350g (12oz) dried spaghetti** + **Freshly ground black pepper**

1

Toast the pine nuts in a dry pan over a medium heat for 2-3 minutes.

2

Pulse the pine nuts, garlic, salt, and basil in a food processor until you have a silky paste.

3

Transfer to a bowl and mix in the cheese.

4

Using a spoon, beat in the olive oil a little at a time until you have a thick sauce.

5

Boil the pasta in a pan of lightly salted water for 8-10 minutes. Reserve a little bit of pasta water, and drain.

6

Return the pasta to the pan and mix in half of the pesto. Add the reserved water to help bind everything together, then add pepper.

Reserved water.

67

1

Place all the ingredients except the oil in a bowl and mix until combined.

15 mins 20 mins Makes 24

2

Roll into 24 balls and cook in a pan over medium heat for 10-12 minutes until browned.

Meatballs

Meatballs are a really versatile ingredient. There are recipes on the following pages that you can use either of these versions with.

Cook the meatballs in two batches so they brown better.

200g (7oz) lean minced beef

+

200g (7oz) minced pork

+

2 tbsp freshly grated Parmesan cheese

+

2 tbsp chopped parsley

+

1 tsp dried oregano

+

1 tbsp dried breadcrumbs

+

1 egg, beaten

+

2 tbsp olive oil

Ingredients

2 tbsp olive oil

1 onion, chopped

1 clove garlic

250g (9oz) mushrooms, finely chopped

1 x 400g (14oz) green lentils, drained and rinsed

6 tbsp dried breadcrumbs

2 tbsp chopped parsley

2 tsp dried mixed herbs

1 egg, beaten

Veggie balls

1

Heat 1 tbsp of oil in a pan and cook the onions, garlic, and mushrooms for 5 minutes.

2

Pulse in a food processor with the rest of the ingredients until combined. Transfer to a bowl and chill for 30 minutes.

3

Roll into 24 balls. Then add the remaining oil to a pan and cook over medium heat for 10-12 minutes, turning often.

 15 mins, plus 30 mins chilling   15 mins   Makes 24

Meatball ciabatta

This delicious, hot sandwich is a fun and creative way to use your meat or veggie balls from pages 68-69.

1

Lightly toast both sides of the bread under the grill.

2

Spread a layer of pizza sauce over one half of the bread.

3

Use either meat or veggie balls.

Arrange the meatballs on top and grill for 2 minutes.

4

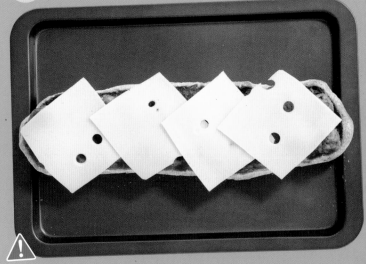

Lay slices of cheese on top and return to the grill for 2-3 minutes. Place the other half of the bread on top and serve.

Ingredients

1 ciabatta, halved
lengthwise

6 tbsp pizza
or pasta sauce

meat or veggie balls
from pages 68-69

4 slices Emmental or
other melting cheese

5 mins · 7 mins · Serves 4

Cut the
sandwich
into four.

Spaghetti & meatballs

Put either your meat or veggie balls from pages 68-69 to good use with this hearty and delicious pasta dish.

5 mins | 30 mins | Serves 4

1

Heat the oil in a large pan and gently cook the onion and garlic for 4-5 minutes.

2

Stir in the tomatoes, passata, oregano, and sugar, then add 200ml (7fl oz) of water and season with salt and pepper.

3

Bring to a boil, then simmer uncovered for 15 minutes. Add the meat or veggie balls and cook for another 7-8 minutes.

Ingredients

 + + +  +

1 tbsp olive oil | 1 onion, sliced | 1 clove garlic, crushed | 1 x 400g (14oz) can chopped tomatoes

4

Meanwhile, cook the pasta in salted water, then use tongs to transfer it into the sauce and combine.

The pasta should be tender but still firm to the bite and not soggy.

Sprinkle with Parmesan.

400ml (14fl oz) passata

1 tsp dried oregano

1 tsp sugar

meat or veggie balls from pages 68-69

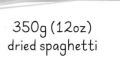
350g (12oz) dried spaghetti

Minty kebabs

The secret to this recipe is the flavourful marinade. If you start this dish a day ahead of time it'll taste even better.

10 mins, plus marinating   15 mins   Makes 4

Fresh mint

Sprinkle feta on top.

Ingredients

 150g (5½oz) natural yogurt

 1 tbsp olive oil

 2 tbsp lemon juice

 4 tbsp freshly chopped mint

1

Mix the yogurt, oil, lemon juice, mint, and paprika in a bowl. Season with salt and pepper.

Soaking wooden skewers stops them burning.

2

Full of flavour!

Add the lamb and stir to coat. Leave in the fridge to marinate for an hour, or overnight.

3

Check page 23 for a tzatziki dip that's perfect with these kebabs.

Thread the lamb onto wooden skewers that have been soaked in water. Set the grill to high and cook the kebabs for 6-7 minutes.

4

Turn the kebabs and brush with the remaining marinade. Cook for another 6-7 minutes or until the meat is cooked through.

1 tsp paprika

350g (12oz) lamb, cut into cubes

50g (1¾oz) feta cheese, crumbled

Ingredients

 +  **+** **+** **+**

1 tbsp dark soy sauce   3 tbsp runny honey   2 tsp wholegrain mustard   2 tsp olive oil

10 mins   40 mins   Serves 4

Sticky chicken

This simple meal is all cooked in one tray, so it's great for a dinner when you're after flavour without the washing up!

Sticky sauce

Goes well with a green salad, but it's delicious on its own, too!

8 boneless, skinless
chirken thighs

+

3 carrots, peeled
and quartered

+

3 parsnips, peeled
and quartered

+

a few sprigs
of thyme

1

Preheat the oven to 200°C (400°F/Gas 6).
Mix the soy, honey, mustard, and oil in a
bowl. Add the chicken and stir.

2

Place the carrots and parsnips in a baking
tray and lay the chicken on top. Season,
add the thyme, and pour the sauce on top.

3

Sticky and delicious!

Roast for 20 minutes,
then remove from the
oven and stir. Return
to the oven and cook
for a further 20 minutes,
or until the chicken is
cooked through.

Spoon any remaining
sauce on top of
the chicken.

77

Ingredients

 1 tbsp olive oil  + 1 onion, chopped +  1 clove garlic, crushed +  1 large potato, peeled and cut into small chunks +  2 carrots, peeled and cut into small chunks +

Chunky vegetable soup

Warming, comforting, and packed with healthy vegetables, this soup is the perfect dish for a cold evening.

Serve with crusty bread.

Lots of chunky veg!

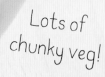
10 mins   30 mins   Serves 4

1 tsp ground paprika	400g (14oz) can chopped tomatoes	1 litre (1¾ pints) hot vegetable stock	200g (7oz) kale or cabbage, thinly sliced	100g (3½oz) green beans, cut into 2.5cm (1in) pieces

You want the onions to turn clear, not brown.

1

Heat the oil in a large saucepan and cook the onion and garlic over a low heat for 3-4 minutes until soft.

2

Add the potatoes and carrots and cook for 2-3 minutes.

3

Stir in the paprika, tomatoes, and stock. Bring to the boil, then cover and simmer for 15 minutes.

4

Add the kale and green beans, then cook for a further 6-7 minutes or until tender. Season to taste and serve.

79

Ingredients

 1 tbsp sunflower oil  + 1 onion, chopped + 1 clove garlic, chopped  + 2 tsp finely grated ginger +

10 mins 25 mins Serves 4

Squash & coconut curry

This yummy one-pot dish is packed with flavour. It's also just as good with sweet potato or pumpkin instead of squash.

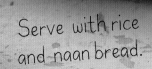
Serve with rice and naan bread.

80

+  +  +

2 tbsp mild curry powder

1 large butternut squash, cubed

1 x 400ml (14fl oz) can coconut milk

225g (8oz) green beans, trimmed and chopped

1

Heat the oil in a large saucepan over medium heat and cook the onion, garlic, and ginger for 2-3 minutes.

2

Add the curry powder and cook for 1 minute.

Mix together

3

Add the butternut squash and 2 tbsp of water and cook for 1-2 minutes, until soft.

4

Pour the coconut milk and 200ml (7fl oz) water on top and stir in the beans. Bring to the boil, then reduce the heat, cover, and simmer for 15-20 minutes.

81

Ingredients

350g (12oz) dried rigatoni or penne pasta

+

2 tbsp olive oil

+

150g (5½oz) pancetta or streaky bacon, chopped

+

1 onion, finely chopped

+

1 clove garlic, crushed

Summer pasta

This simple pasta is a real breeze to make. The cherry tomatoes burst to help create the pasta sauce.

1

"Al dente" pasta is cooked but still a little firm.

Boil the pasta in salted water for about 8-10 minutes, or according to packet instructions, until al dente.

2

Meanwhile, heat the oil in a large frying pan and add the pancetta, onion, and garlic. Cook for 4-5 minutes.

3

Stir in the tomatoes, sugar, and chilli flakes if using. Cook for 5-6 minutes, stirring often, until the tomatoes start to burst.

500g (1lb 2oz)
cherry tomatoes

+

1 tsp sugar

+

pinch of dried chilli
flakes, optional

+

10 basil leaves,
shredded

4

You can also
top with
Parmesan.

Drain the pasta and reserve
a little of the cooking water.
Add the pasta and basil to
the pan, and toss well. If
the mix is too thick, stir in
a little pasta water.

Rigatoni pasta
is great for
holding sauce.

5 mins   12 mins   Serves 4

Tomato soup

This soup is really fresh and easy. Best of all, it all happens in a few minutes in one pan. It's "soup-er simple!"

Fresh basil pairs well with tomatoes.

Ingredients

 + + + + + + +

1 tbsp olive oil

1 small onion, chopped

1 clove garlic

2 x 400g (14oz) cans peeled whole tomatoes

2 tbsp tomato purée

1

You want the onions to turn soft but not brown.

Heat the oil in a pan and cook the onions and garlic on a low heat for about 5 minutes.

2

Stir in the tomatoes, tomato purée, sugar, and stock. Bring to a boil then reduce the heat and simmer for 5 mins.

3

Use a blender or stick blender to blitz the soup until smooth. Season to taste and garnish with basil leaves.

Canned tomatoes

🍅 Fresh tomatoes are only at their best for a short time each year, but good quality canned versions allow us to have ripe tomatoes all year round.

🍅 Canned tomatoes come either whole or chopped. You can also buy passata, which is blended tomatoes.

1 tsp sugar   300ml (10fl oz) hot vegetable stock   handful of fresh basil leaves

Ingredients

1 large roasting chicken about 2kg (4½lb)

+

1 tbsp olive oil

+

2 onions, cut into quarters

+

2 sticks celery, chopped

Roast chicken

15 mins | 2 hours | Serves 6

Roasting a chicken is simple and economical. Any leftovers you have can be used in recipes on the following pages.

Crispy skin!

fresh herbs, such as thyme, rosemary, bay

1 lemon

1

Preheat the oven to 220°C (425°F/Gas 7). Rub the chicken with oil and season with salt and pepper.

Chicken tips:

For best results, remove the chicken from the fridge 30 minutes before cooking. This will help the chicken to cook evenly.

Always thoroughly wash your hands with hot, soapy water after touching raw chicken.

While the chicken rests, add stock and a few teaspoons of flour to the tray and stir to create a gravy.

2

Place the onions, celery, and chicken in a roasting tray. Squeeze the lemon on top and place in the cavity with the herbs. Pour 200ml (7fl oz) water into the roasting tray.

3

Roast for 15 minutes, then reduce the temperature to 180°C (350°F/Gas 4) and cook for about 90 minutes. Allow to rest for 20 minutes while you make a gravy.

Chicken & mango salad

A fresh, healthy salad is a great way to use up leftover cooked chicken. This version comes with a zingy, fruity dressing.

10 mins Serves 2

Zingy dressing

Ingredients

 + + + +

1 ripe mango   1 ripe avocado   125g (4½oz) leftover chicken from page 86   ¼ cucumber, sliced

1

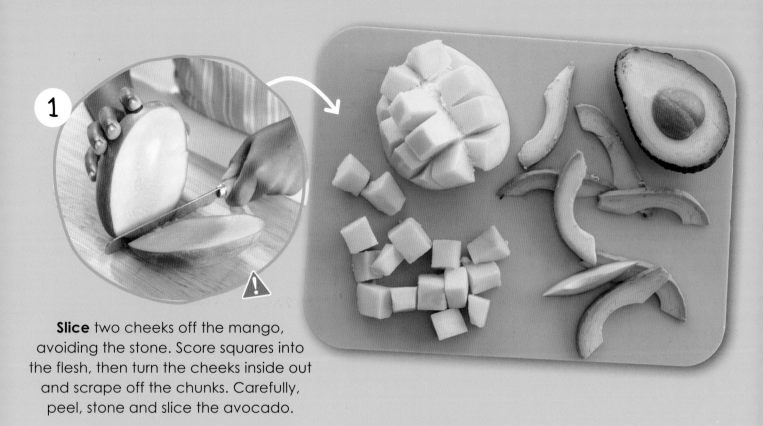

Slice two cheeks off the mango, avoiding the stone. Score squares into the flesh, then turn the cheeks inside out and scrape off the chunks. Carefully, peel, stone and slice the avocado.

2

Mix the dressing ingredients together. Place all the salad ingredients except the mixed leaves into a bowl and pour the dressing on top. Mix and serve on a bed of mixed leaves.

For the dressing:
- grated zest of 1 lime
- 2 tbsp lime juice
- 1 tbsp soy sauce
- 1 tbsp honey
- 2 tsp freshly grated ginger

+ 2 tbsp chopped coriander

+ 100g (3½oz) mixed salad leaves

Chicken noodle soup

This is another way to use up leftover chicken from page 86. You can add almost any vegetables you like, too.

When liquid is simmering it should bubble lightly.

1

Place the stock, onions, and soy sauce in a large pan and bring to the boil. Reduce the heat to a simmer.

2

Add the noodles and carrots and simmer for a further 2 minutes.

3

Stir in the mangetout, corn, and chicken and simmer for 3-4 minutes, until the noodles and vegetables are tender.

Ingredients

 +  + +

1.2 litres (2 pints) hot chicken stock

4 spring onions, sliced

1 tsp dark soy sauce

250g (9oz) cooked egg noodles

4 **Ladle** the soup into bowls and serve immediately.

Comforting and healthy!

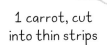
1 carrot, cut into thin strips

125g (4½oz) mangetout

100g (3½oz) canned sweetcorn

200g (7oz) leftover shredded chicken from page 86

Sweet treats and bakes

Everybody likes a treat every now and then, and these savoury bakes and sweet delights will always hit the spot.

Ingredients

2 lemons + 275g (9½oz) self-raising flour + ½ tsp baking soda + ½ tsp salt + 100g (3½oz) caster sugar +

Lemon muffins

These bright, zingy muffins are a real treat.
They're light and fluffy, but packed with flavour.

1 Preheat the oven to 190°C (375°F/Gas 5). Line a muffin tin with 8 muffin cases.

Dry ingredients

2 Juice and grate one lemon and retain the juice. Add the zest to a bowl with the flour, baking soda, salt, sugar, and poppy seeds.

Wet ingredients

3 Beat the milk, egg, oil, and lemon juice in a jug, then pour the wet ingredients into the dry and stir until just combined.

4 Spoon into the cases and cook in the oven for 20-25 minutes until well risen. Leave to cool for a few minutes.

2 tbsp poppy seeds   150ml (5fl oz) milk   1 egg, beaten   90ml (3fl oz) sunflower oil

5

For the icing:
- 75g (2½ oz) icing sugar
- 2 tsp lemon zest
- 2 tsp lemon juice

Decorate with grated lemon zest or jellied lemon slices.

Once the muffins have cooled, make the icing and drizzle it over the muffins.

10 mins   25 mins   Makes 8

Ingredients

 250g (9oz) rolled oats

+

 100g (3½oz) almonds, roughly chopped

+

 75g (2½oz) mixed seeds (sunflower, pumpkin, sesame)

+

 100g (3½oz) runny honey

Granola bars

15 mins   25 mins   Makes 16

These chunky treats are great for breakfast or as a quick snack. The peanut butter and dates make them really soft and chewy!

Store any leftover bars in an airtight container.

+

125g (4½oz)
peanut butter

+

100g (3½oz)
pitted dates

+
100g (3½oz) dried mixed berries
(blueberries, cherries, cranberries) or raisins

1

Preheat the oven to 180°C (350°F/Gas 4). Lightly oil a 28x18cm (11x7in) tray and add the oats, almonds, and seeds. Cook for 10-12 minutes.

2

Warm the honey and peanut butter in a pan over a low heat. Stir occasionally, until combined.

3

Place the dates, 4 tbsp of warm water, and the honey mixture in a food processor, and blend until smooth.

4

Allow to cool slightly, then cut into bars and leave to set in the tin.

Mix the date and oat mixtures in a bowl with the berries and stir until combined. Spoon into a tin and flatten with the back of a spoon. Cook for 12 minutes.

Easiest flatbreads ever

These flatbreads are ready to eat in minutes, and are incredibly delicious brushed with garlic butter.

You can also add parsley to the melted butter.

Chopped parsley

5 mins   4 mins each   Makes 12

Ingredients

350g (12oz)
plain flour

+

1 tsp
baking powder

+

½ tsp salt

+

350g (12oz)
natural yogurt

+

melted garlic
butter, to finish

1

Rough dough

Place the flour, baking powder, salt, and yogurt in a bowl and mix together until roughly combined.

2

Flour stops the dough from sticking.

Lightly dust a surface with flour, then knead the mixture for about 2 minutes to make a smooth dough.

3

Cut the dough in half, then cut each half into six pieces. Roll the pieces into balls, then roll out on a floured surface until 3mm (⅛in) thick.

4

⚠️

Place a griddle pan over a high heat and cook the flatbreads for 1-2 minutes each side, until puffed up.

99

Focaccia

This dimpled Italian bread can be flavoured with herbs, cheese, tomatoes or olives. Follow this basic recipe or add your favourite ingredients.

15 mins plus 2 hrs rising   20 mins   Serves 8

Best served warm, dipped in olive oil.

Ingredients

 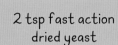

350g (12oz) strong white bread flour + 2 tsp fast action dried yeast + 1 tsp salt + 250ml (8fl oz) lukewarm water + 4 tbsp olive oil

1

Sift the flour into a large bowl and stir in the yeast and salt. Lightly oil a 28x18cm (11x7in) rectangular tin.

2

Make a well in the centre and add the water and oil. Mix until it starts to come together and forms a smooth dough.

3

Knead on a clean surface for 10 minutes until smooth and elastic, then cover in a clean bowl and leave to rise for 1 hour.

4

Press the dough into the tin so it fills all the corners. Cover with cling film and leave to rise for an hour.

5

To finish:
- 1 tbsp olive oil
- sprigs of rosemary
- sea salt for sprinkling

Dimples

Meanwhile, preheat the oven to 200°C (400°F/Gas 6). Then use your fingertips to make dimples over the bread and top with oil, rosemary, and salt. Bake for 20-25 minutes until golden and crispy.

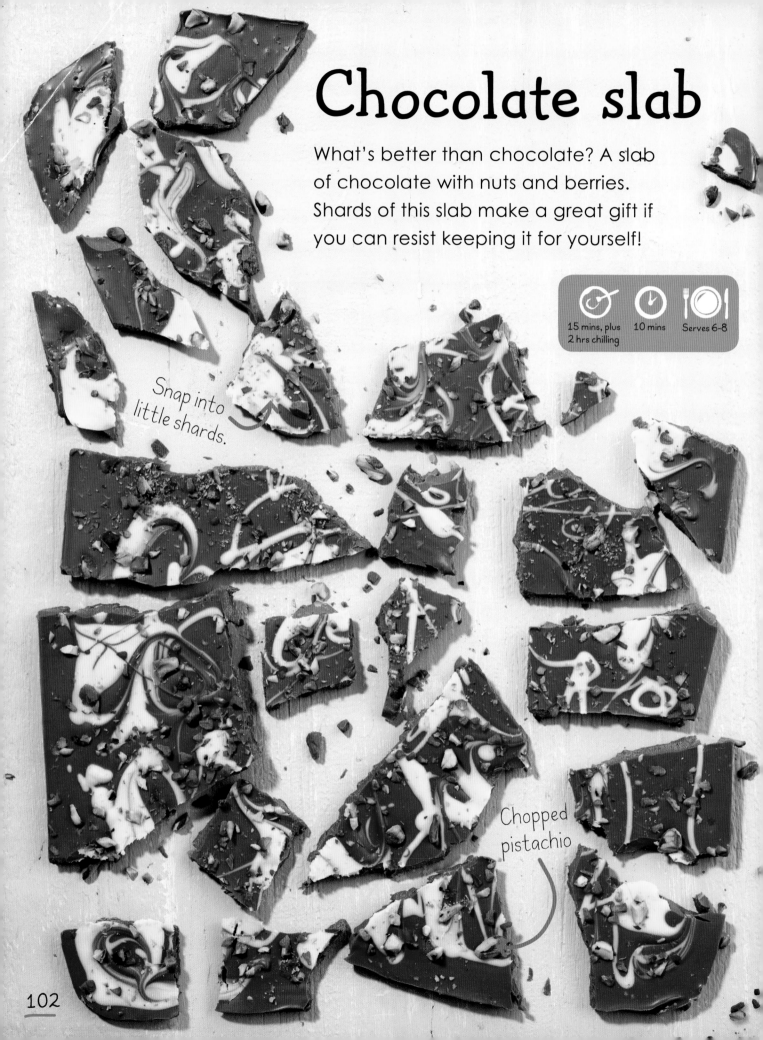

Chocolate slab

What's better than chocolate? A slab of chocolate with nuts and berries. Shards of this slab make a great gift if you can resist keeping it for yourself!

15 mins, plus 2 hrs chilling · 10 mins · Serves 6-8

Snap into little shards.

Chopped pistachio

Ingredients

600g (1lb 5oz) milk chocolate, broken into pieces

+

200g (7oz) white chocolate, broken into pieces

+

selection of chopped nuts, dried fruit, or freeze dried raspberries

1

Lightly brush a 33x23cm (13x9in) baking tray or shallow tin with oil, then line with baking paper.

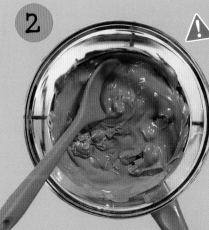

2

⚠️

Place the milk chocolate in a large heatproof bowl over a pan of simmering water. Melt the chocolate, stirring as you go.

3

Pour the melted chocolate into the tin, tipping it from side to side to fill the corners.

4

Melt the white chocolate as before, then pour small amounts into the tin and make swirly patterns with a cocktail stick.

5

Scatter with your desired toppings, then leave to set in the fridge for about 2 hours.

You can also make mini versions in a muffin tin.

Ingredients

175g (6oz) unsalted
butter, softened

175g (6oz)
caster sugar

3 medium
eggs, beaten

grated zest
of an orange

1 tsp baking powder

175g (6oz)
self-raising flour

104

Orange cake

This easy sponge cake recipe is made
by the all-in-one method, where all
the ingredients are whisked together.

Decorate
with orange
zest.

Sweet
filling

For the filling:
- 75g (2½ oz)
unsalted butter,
softened
- 250g (9oz) icing
sugar, sifted
- 2 tbsp orange juice
- grated zest
of 1 orange

10 mins   30 mins   Serves 8

1 Preheat the oven to 180°C (350°F/Gas 4). Grease two 20cm (8in) cake tins and line the bases with baking paper.

2 Gather all the ingredients and beat together with an electric whisk until thick and well-mixed.

3 Divide the mix between the tins and level the tops. Bake in the oven for 25-30 minutes.

4 Leave to cool in the tins for 5 minutes, then turn out onto a rack and allow to cool fully.

5 To make the filling, mix the butter, icing sugar, orange zest, and orange juice in a bowl until smooth and creamy.

6 Spread half the filling on the base side of one of the cakes. Lay the other cake on top and spread the remaining filling over it.

Ingredients

 + + + +

| 100g (3½oz) butter, cut into cubes | 900g (2lb) Bramley apples, peeled, cored and sliced | 100g (3½oz) demerara sugar | 2 tbsp apple juice |

10 mins   45 mins   Serves 6-8

Apple crumble

A classic dessert that's as simple as it is delicious. The best thing about a crumble is the mix of crunchy topping and soft filling.

Serve with either ice-cream or custard.

Crunchy topping

100g (3½oz)
plain flour

125g (4½oz) rolled
jumbo oats

4 tbsp mixed seeds, such
as sunflower and pumpkin

1 tsp ground
cinnamon

The sugar will turn into
a syrup when it cooks.

1

Preheat the oven to 180°C (350°F/Gas 4).
Melt 25g (scant 1oz) of butter in a pan
and stir in the apples, half the sugar, and
apple juice.

2

Cook for 5-6 minutes, covered, then
spoon the apple mixture into a 1 litre
(1¾ pints) ovenproof dish.

3

Place the flour in a bowl and rub in the
remaining butter with your fingertips until
the mixture looks like breadcrumbs. Stir
in the oats, sugar, seeds, and cinnamon.

4

Spoon the mixture over the top of the
apples. Bake for 30-40 minutes until
the topping is golden.

10 mins, plus 3 hrs freezing time | 10 mins | Serves 4

Raspberry ice

This dessert is colourful, zingy, and refreshing. You can switch out the raspberries for other fruits if you like.

Spoon into small glasses or bowls.

Serve immediately

Ingredients

 125g (4½oz) caster sugar

 200ml (7fl oz) cold water

 450g (1lb) fresh raspberries

 2 tbsp lime juice

1

Bring the sugar and water to the boil, then reduce and simmer for 5 minutes until you have a syrup. Allow to cool.

2

Place the raspberries and lime juice in a food processor and blend until you have a thick purée.

3

Add the mixture to a sieve over a bowl. Use a spoon to press the mixture through the sieve, then discard the seeds.

4

Pour the cooled syrup into the raspberry mixture, then pour into a shallow plastic box and freeze for 2 hours.

5

Remove from the freezer and scrape with a fork, mixing the solid mixture into the liquid mixture.

6

Before serving, transfer to the fridge for 20 minutes to soften.

Return to the freezer and repeat the process twice more at 30 minute intervals, then let it freeze a final time.

Ingredients

100g (3½oz)
butter, softened

125g (4½oz)
caster sugar

1 egg

½ tsp vanilla extract

150g (5½oz)
self-raising flour

110

Clever cookies

By adding a few different ingredients to this basic dough, you can have a variety of tasty treats. How clever is that?

Cranberry and white chocolate

Blueberry and lemon

Cinnamon and raisin

Chocolate chunk

10 mins   15 mins   Makes 18

1

Preheat the oven to 180°C (350°F/Gas 4) and line two baking sheets with baking paper.

2

Cream the butter and sugar together with an electric whisk, then beat in the egg and vanilla extract.

3

Using a metal spoon, stir in the flour and any extra ingredients (see next page) and mix together.

4

Roll the dough into about 18 balls and place on the baking sheets, leaving a little space around them. Flatten slightly and cook for 12-15 minutes.

There are some great ingredient suggestions on the next page.

Cinnamon & raisin

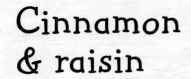

1 tsp ground cinnamon

+

125g (4½oz) raisins

Chocolate chunks

75g (2½oz) dark chocolate chunks

You can use chocolate chips if you prefer!

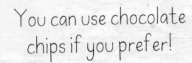

+

75g (2½oz) white chocolate chunks

White chocolate & cranberry

75g (2½oz)
dried cranberries

+

100g (3½oz) white
chocolate chunks

Lemon & blueberry

2 tsp grated
lemon zest

+

100g (3½oz) fresh blueberries

Ingredients

 75g (2½oz) butter + 150g (5½oz) digestive biscuits, crushed + 200g (7oz) white chocolate + 500g (1lb 2oz) marscapone cheese +

Cheesecake

This rich dessert is packed with flavour, and works just as well with raspberries or strawberries.

20 mins, plus 30 mins chilling | 15 mins | Serves 8

Put the biscuits in a plastic bag and crush them with a rolling pin.

1

Melt the butter in a pan and stir in the biscuits. Press into the base of a 20cm (8in) loose-bottomed cake tin.

2

Meanwhile melt the chocolate in a bowl over a pan of simmering water, stirring occasionally, until dissolved.

3

Beat until smooth

Beat the marscapone and icing sugar with an electric whisk and mix in the chocolate.

4

Smooth the mixture over the buttery biscuit base and chill for about 30 minutes, until set.

25g (scant 1oz)
icing sugar, sifted

+

250g (9oz)
fresh blackberries

+

50g (1¾oz)
caster sugar

+

1 tsp cornflour

+

2 tsp lemon juice

5

Meanwhile, cook the blackberries and sugar in a saucepan over low heat for 2 minutes, stirring until the sugar dissolves.

6

Mix the cornflour and lemon juice and stir it into to the blackberries. Cook for 2-3 minutes, then drizzle over the cheesecake base.

Top with grated white chocolate.

Chocolate mug brownies

These brownies are rich, gooey, and only take a few minutes to make in a microwave. What's not to love?

Serve warm with a scoop of ice cream.

Mix the dry ingredients in a 200ml (7fl oz) microwavable cup or mug.

1

Ingredients

2 tbsp plain flour

+

2 tbsp soft brown sugar

+

1 tbsp cocoa powder

+

pinch of salt

Stir in the oil and milk until there are no lumps, then mix in the chocolate chunks or chips.

2

1 tbsp sunflower oil

+

2 tbsp milk

+

1 tbsp chocolate chunks or chips

3

On a 1000w (E) microwave, cook on high for 1 minute. Allow to stand for 30 seconds.

117

Smoothies

Nothing beats a fruity smoothie on a hot day. Here are four quick recipes, but experiment and make your own.

Mango & banana

flesh of 1 ripe mango

+

1 small banana, chopped

+

300ml (10fl oz) orange juice or coconut water

Full of flavour!

Purple berry

300ml (10fl oz) apple juice

+

75g (2½oz) blueberries

+

75g (2½oz) blackberries

+

1 small banana, chopped

1 **Place** all the ingredients and a few ice cubes in a blender and blitz until smooth. ⚠

2 **Add** a little more water, milk or juice for the desired consistency.

3 **Pour** into glasses or chill in the fridge. Drink and enjoy!

Berry & vanilla

75g (2½oz) strawberries, roughly chopped

+

75g (2½oz) raspberries

+ 200g (7oz) vanilla yogurt + 100ml (3½fl oz) milk

Super green

2 kiwis, peeled and chopped

+

1 apple, cored, peeled and chopped

juice of 1 lime

+

200ml (7fl oz) cold water

+

50g (1¾oz) fresh spinach

5 mins   Serves 2

Kitchen terms

Don't worry if you come across a word in this book that you don't understand, these explanations should help you out.

Al dente
Pasta that is cooked through but still slightly firm when bitten.

Bake
Cooking food in an oven.

Beat
Stirring ingredients quickly using a whisk, fork, or spoon until it makes a smooth mixture.

Blend
Mixing ingredients together in a blender or food processor until combined.

Boil
Cooking liquid in a pan over high temperature so that it bubbles strongly.

Chill
Placing ingredients or a dish in the fridge to cool down or keep cool.

Combine
Mixing several ingredients together.

Chop
Using a knife to cut ingredients into smaller pieces.

Core
Removing the centre of a piece of fruit to take out the seeds.

Cream
Quickly combining butter and sugar together to create a light, fluffy mixture.

Dice
Cutting an ingredient into small, equal cubes.

Drain
Removing excess liquid by pouring ingredients through a colander or strainer, or by resting on kitchen paper.

Drizzle
Pouring a small amount of liquid, such as olive oil or salad dressing over a dish.

Fold
Using a spatula to gently mix ingredients together so that they stay light and fluffy.

Grate
Shredding an ingredient into little pieces by rubbing it against a grater.

Grease
Spreading a layer of butter or oil on a tin to stop ingredients from sticking to it.

Grill
Cooking food from one direction, usually using high heat.

Juice
Squeezing the liquid out of fruits or vegetables.

Knead

Working a dough by stretching and pulling until it becomes smooth and elastic.

Line

Placing baking paper or foil in a tin so that food won't stick to it.

Marinate

Soaking ingredients in a flavourful liquid to add flavour.

Mash

Crushing ingredients with a fork or potato masher.

Mix

Combining ingredients together, either by hand or with equipment.

Preheat

Turning the oven on 15 minutes before it is needed so that it reaches the recommended temperature before the food goes in.

Roll

Flattening out and shaping dough or pastry using a rolling pin.

Rub in

Rubbing flour and butter together with your fingers to create a texture that is similar to breadcrumbs.

Score

Making shallow cuts across the surface of an ingredient.

Season

Adding salt, pepper, vinegar, or other spices to a dish to add flavour.

Set

Leaving food on the worktop, in the fridge, or in the freezer until it firms up and turns solid.

Sift

Using a sieve to remove lumps from dry ingredients such as flour.

Simmer

Cooking a liquid over a low heat, so that it bubbles gently.

Slicing

Using a knife to cut food into strips.

Stone

Remove the stone from fruit or vegetables.

Stir-fry

Cooking ingredients in a pan very quickly over high heat whilst stirring.

Strain

See "drain".

Whisk

Whipping up ingredients using a whisk. Used to introduce air into the mixture.

Useful skills

There are some cooking techniques that you'll use over and over again. Follow these steps to learn these skills and you'll be an expert in no time!

Cooking fluffy rice

The perfect rice is light and fluffy. This simple method works every time.

1. Measure out a ratio of 1 part rice to 1.5 parts cold water. Wash the rice under cold water until it runs clear, then add to a saucepan.

2. Bring to a boil, then cover and reduce to a simmer. Cook for 10 minutes, then turn off the heat and leave to steam, covered, for another 10 minutes.

Making stock

Stock from a shop or made from a cube is really handy, but if you've got time, the homemade version is much better.

1. Add chopped onions, carrots, celery, herbs, seasoning, and leftover chicken, including the bones, to a pan. (Leave the chicken out if you want to make vegetable stock).

2. Cover with cold water and bring to a boil. Reduce the heat and simmer for 2-3 hours, skimming off any froth as you go.

3. Strain the stock through a sieve and allow to cool. Store in the fridge or freezer.

Prepping avocado

Avocado is a great addition to many dishes, but it can be tricky to get the stone out if you've never done it before.

1. Place the avocado onto a chopping board and carefully slice it lengthways, all the way round, avoiding the stone.

2. Twist the avocado to separate it into two halves, then use a spoon to remove the stone.

3. Scoop out the flesh with a spoon and either slice it into pieces or mash it with a fork.

Rolling out pastry

Good quality shop-bought pastry is a great time-saver. All you need to do is roll it out.

1 Sprinkle flour onto a rolling pin and your work surface. Use the rolling pin to push down and forward over the pastry, using long, steady strokes.

2 Turn the pastry around and repeat as necessary, until it reaches your desired thickness.

Separating eggs

Some recipes only require the egg white or yolk. Luckily, it's easy to separate them.

1 Crack an egg on the side of a bowl. Transfer the yolk back and forth from one half of the shell to the other, letting the white fall into the bowl and holding the yolk in the shell.

Shredding chicken

Shredded, leftover chicken can be used in lots of other dishes. It's a great way to get the most out of your ingredients.

1 Wait for the cooked chicken to cool thoroughly and use one fork to hold it still and another to pull it apart. Alternatively, slice the breasts off the carcass and pulse them in a food processor.

Dicing onions

Onions are used in lots of recipes, so learning how to dice one is a skill worth knowing.

1 Peel the onion and slice it in half from root to stem.

2 Make several vertical slices toward the root, being careful not to cut all the way to the end.

3 Repeat with horizontal cuts, then hold the onion together and slice down across the cuts you made earlier.

Lining a cake tin

Lining a tin will stop your cake from sticking to it, making it easier to remove.

1 Grease the tin by spreading a layer of oil or butter onto the base and sides.

2 Place the tin on baking paper and draw around the edges, leaving a little extra on all sides.

3 Cut the paper out and press it into the tin. Fold at the corners and snip off any excess.

Kneading dough

Kneading dough can be quite a physical job, but at least it will make you strong!

1 Place the dough onto a floured surface. Using clean hands, stretch the dough by pushing it down and away from you with the heel of your hands.

2 Fold the dough back toward you. Rotate and repeat for 5-10 minutes until the dough has become smooth and elastic.

Weights and measures

All the quantities for ingredients you'll need in this book are written right on the page, but this chart will be handy as you grow as a cook.

A guide to measures

The type of measurements you use depends on the country you live in. We've listed both types here so that if you want to adjust the recipes in this book, or any others you find, you'll have this helpful chart.

Weights

10g	(¼oz)	150g	(5½oz)	800g	(1¾lb)
15g	(½oz)	175g	(6oz)	900g	(2lb)
20g	(¾oz)	200g	(7oz)	1kg	(2¼lb)
25g	(scant 1oz)	225g	(8oz)	1.1kg	(2½lb)
30g	(1oz)	250g	(9oz)	1.25kg	(2¾lb)
45g	(1½oz)	300g	(10oz)	1.35kg	(3lb)
50g	(1¾oz)	350g	(12oz)	1.5kg	(3lb 3oz)
60g	(2oz)	400g	(14oz)	1.8kg	(4lb)
75g	(2½oz)	450g	(1lb)	2kg	(4½lb)
85g	(3oz)	500g	(1lb 2oz)	2.25kg	(5lb)
100g	(3½oz)	550g	(1¼lb)	2.5kg	(5½lb)
115g	(4oz)	600g	(1lb 5oz)	2.7kg	(6lb)
125g	(4½oz)	675g	(1½lb)	3kg	(6½lb)
140g	(5oz)	750g	(1lb 10oz)		

Volume measures

3 tsp = 1 tbsp

4 tbsp	(2fl oz)	200ml	(7fl oz)	450ml	(15fl oz)
75ml	(2½fl oz)	240ml	(8fl oz)	500ml	(16fl oz)
90ml	(3fl oz)	250ml	(9fl oz)	600ml	(1 pint)
100ml	(3½fl oz)	300ml	(10fl oz)	750ml	(1¼ pints)
120ml	(4fl oz)	350ml	(12fl oz)	900ml	(1½ pints)
150ml	(5fl oz)	400ml	(14fl oz)	1 litre	(1¾ pints)

Oven temperatures

130°C	(250°F/Gas ½)
140°C	(275°F/Gas 1)
150°C	(300°F/Gas 2)
160°C	(325°F/Gas 3)
180°C	(350°F/Gas 4)
190°C	(375°F/Gas 5)
200°C	(400°F/Gas 6)
220°C	(425°F/Gas 7)
230°C	(450°F/Gas 8)
240°C	(475°F/Gas 9)

Index

Acknowledgements

The publisher would like to thank the following
for their kind permission to reproduce their photographs:

(Key: a-above; b-below/bottom; c-centre; f-far; l-left;
r-right; t-top)

6-7 Dreamstime.com: Liubirong. **8-9 Dreamstime.com:**
Liubirong. **10 Dreamstime.com:** Konstantin Kirillov /
Kvkirillov (crb). **11 123RF.com:** Zoran Mladenovic /
feelphotoart (tc). **120-121 Dreamstime.com:** Liubirong.
124-125 Dreamstime.com: Liubirong. **126-127 Dreamstime.
com:** Liubirong. **128 Dreamstime.com:** Liubirong

All other images © Dorling Kindersley
For further information see: www.dkimages.com

DK would like to thank James Tye for additional
photography, Marie Lorimer for indexing, Eleanor
Bates, Lynne Murray, Saksh Saluja, and Romaine
Werblow for picture library assistance, and Rachael
Hare, Violet Peto, and Artie King for help during
the photoshoots.